Table of Contents

List of Figures

List of Tables

Executive Summary

The national and economic security of the United States depends on the reliable functioning of critical infrastructure. Cybersecurity threats exploit the increased complexity and connectivity of critical infrastructure systems, placing the Nation's security, economy, and public safety and health at risk. Similar to financial and reputational risk, cybersecurity risk affects a company's bottom line. It can drive up costs and impact revenue. It can harm an organization's ability to innovate and to gain and maintain customers.

To better address these risks, the President issued Executive Order 13636, "Improving Critical Infrastructure Cybersecurity," on February 12, 2013, which established that "[i]t is the Policy of the United States to enhance the security and resilience of the Nation's critical infrastructure and to maintain a cyber environment that encourages efficiency, innovation, and economic prosperity while promoting safety, security, business confidentiality, privacy, and civil liberties." In enacting this policy, the Executive Order calls for the development of a voluntary risk-based Cybersecurity Framework – a set of industry standards and best practices to help organizations manage cybersecurity risks. The resulting Framework, created through collaboration between government and the private sector, uses a common language to address and manage cybersecurity risk in a cost-effective way based on business needs without placing additional regulatory requirements on businesses.

The Framework focuses on using business drivers to guide cybersecurity activities and considering cybersecurity risks as part of the organization's risk management processes. The Framework consists of three parts: the Framework Core, the Framework Profile, and the Framework Implementation Tiers. The Framework Core is a set of cybersecurity activities, outcomes, and informative references that are common across critical infrastructure sectors, providing the detailed guidance for developing individual organizational Profiles. Through use of the Profiles, the Framework will help the organization align its cybersecurity activities with its business requirements, risk tolerances, and resources. The Tiers provide a mechanism for organizations to view and understand the characteristics of their approach to managing cybersecurity risk.

The Executive Order also requires that the Framework include a methodology to protect individual privacy and civil liberties when critical infrastructure organizations conduct cybersecurity activities. While processes and existing needs will differ, the Framework can assist organizations in incorporating privacy and civil liberties as part of a comprehensive cybersecurity program.

The Framework enables organizations – regardless of size, degree of cybersecurity risk, or cybersecurity sophistication – to apply the principles and best practices of risk management to improving the security and resilience of critical infrastructure. The Framework provides organization and structure to today's multiple approaches to cybersecurity by assembling standards, guidelines, and practices that are working effectively in industry today. Moreover, because it references globally recognized standards for cybersecurity, the Framework can also be used by organizations located outside the United States and can serve as a model for international cooperation on strengthening critical infrastructure cybersecurity.

The Framework is not a one-size-fits-all approach to managing cybersecurity risk for critical infrastructure. Organizations will continue to have unique risks – different threats, different vulnerabilities, different risk tolerances – and how they implement the practices in the Framework will vary. Organizations can determine activities that are important to critical service delivery and can prioritize investments to maximize the impact of each dollar spent. Ultimately, the Framework is aimed at reducing and better managing cybersecurity risks.

The Framework is a living document and will continue to be updated and improved as industry provides feedback on implementation. As the Framework is put into practice, lessons learned will be integrated into future versions. This will ensure it is meeting the needs of critical infrastructure owners and operators in a dynamic and challenging environment of new threats, risks, and solutions.

Use of this voluntary Framework is the next step to improve the cybersecurity of our Nation's critical infrastructure – providing guidance for individual organizations, while increasing the cybersecurity posture of the Nation's critical infrastructure as a whole.

1.0   Framework Introduction

The national and economic security of the United States depends on the reliable functioning of critical infrastructure. To strengthen the resilience of this infrastructure, President Obama issued Executive Order 13636 (EO), "Improving Critical Infrastructure Cybersecurity," on February 12, 2013.[1] This Executive Order calls for the development of a voluntary Cybersecurity Framework ("Framework") that provides a "prioritized, flexible, repeatable, performance-based, and cost-effective approach" to manage cybersecurity risk for those processes, information, and systems directly involved in the delivery of critical infrastructure services. The Framework, developed in collaboration with industry, provides guidance to an organization on managing cybersecurity risk.

Critical infrastructure is defined in the EO as "systems and assets, whether physical or virtual, so vital to the United States that the incapacity or destruction of such systems and assets would have a debilitating impact on security, national economic security, national public health or safety, or any combination of those matters." Due to the increasing pressures from external and internal threats, organizations responsible for critical infrastructure need to have a consistent and iterative approach to identifying, assessing, and managing cybersecurity risk. This approach is necessary regardless of an organization's size, threat exposure, or cybersecurity sophistication today.

The critical infrastructure community includes public and private owners and operators, and other entities with a role in securing the Nation's infrastructure. Members of each critical infrastructure sector perform functions that are supported by information technology (IT) and industrial control systems (ICS).[2] This reliance on technology, communication, and the interconnectivity of IT and ICS has changed and expanded the potential vulnerabilities and increased potential risk to operations. For example, as ICS and the data produced in ICS operations are increasingly used to deliver critical services and support business decisions, the potential impacts of a cybersecurity incident on an organization's business, assets, health and safety of individuals, and the environment should be considered. To manage cybersecurity risks, a clear understanding of the organization's business drivers and security considerations specific to its use of IT and ICS is required. Because each organization's risk is unique, along with its use of IT and ICS, the tools and methods used to achieve the outcomes described by the Framework will vary.

Recognizing the role that the protection of privacy and civil liberties plays in creating greater public trust, the Executive Order requires that the Framework include a methodology to protect individual privacy and civil liberties when critical infrastructure organizations conduct cybersecurity activities. Many organizations already have processes for addressing privacy and civil liberties. The methodology is designed to complement such processes and provide guidance to facilitate privacy risk management consistent with an organization's approach to cybersecurity risk management. Integrating privacy and cybersecurity can benefit organizations by increasing customer confidence, enabling more standardized sharing of information, and simplifying operations across legal regimes.

---

[1] Executive Order no. 13636, *Improving Critical Infrastructure Cybersecurity*, DCPD-201300091, February 12, 2013. http://www.gpo.gov/fdsys/pkg/FR-2013-02-19/pdf/2013-03915.pdf

[2] The DHS Critical Infrastructure program provides a listing of the sectors and their associated critical functions and value chains. http://www.dhs.gov/critical-infrastructure-sectors

To ensure extensibility and enable technical innovation, the Framework is technology neutral. The Framework relies on a variety of existing standards, guidelines, and practices to enable critical infrastructure providers to achieve resilience. By relying on those global standards, guidelines, and practices developed, managed, and updated by industry, the tools and methods available to achieve the Framework outcomes will scale across borders, acknowledge the global nature of cybersecurity risks, and evolve with technological advances and business requirements. The use of existing and emerging standards will enable economies of scale and drive the development of effective products, services, and practices that meet identified market needs. Market competition also promotes faster diffusion of these technologies and practices and realization of many benefits by the stakeholders in these sectors.

Building from those standards, guidelines, and practices, the Framework provides a common taxonomy and mechanism for organizations to:

1) Describe their current cybersecurity posture;

2) Describe their target state for cybersecurity;

3) Identify and prioritize opportunities for improvement within the context of a continuous and repeatable process;

4) Assess progress toward the target state;

5) Communicate among internal and external stakeholders about cybersecurity risk.

The Framework complements, and does not replace, an organization's risk management process and cybersecurity program. The organization can use its current processes and leverage the Framework to identify opportunities to strengthen and communicate its management of cybersecurity risk while aligning with industry practices. Alternatively, an organization without an existing cybersecurity program can use the Framework as a reference to establish one.

Just as the Framework is not industry-specific, the common taxonomy of standards, guidelines, and practices that it provides also is not country-specific. Organizations outside the United States may also use the Framework to strengthen their own cybersecurity efforts, and the Framework can contribute to developing a common language for international cooperation on critical infrastructure cybersecurity.

1.1   Overview of the Framework

The Framework is a risk-based approach to managing cybersecurity risk, and is composed of three parts: the Framework Core, the Framework Implementation Tiers, and the Framework Profiles. Each Framework component reinforces the connection between business drivers and cybersecurity activities. These components are explained below.

- The *Framework Core* is a set of cybersecurity activities, desired outcomes, and applicable references that are common across critical infrastructure sectors. The Core presents industry standards, guidelines, and practices in a manner that allows for communication of cybersecurity activities and outcomes across the organization from the executive level to the implementation/operations level. The Framework Core consists of five concurrent and continuous Functions—Identify, Protect, Detect, Respond, Recover. When considered together, these Functions provide a high-level, strategic view of the lifecycle of an organization's management of cybersecurity risk. The Framework Core then identifies underlying key Categories and Subcategories for each Function, and matches them with example Informative References such as existing standards, guidelines, and practices for each Subcategory.

- *Framework Implementation Tiers* ("Tiers") provide context on how an organization views cybersecurity risk and the processes in place to manage that risk. Tiers describe the degree to which an organization's cybersecurity risk management practices exhibit the characteristics defined in the Framework (e.g., risk and threat aware, repeatable, and adaptive). The Tiers characterize an organization's practices over a range, from Partial (Tier 1) to Adaptive (Tier 4). These Tiers reflect a progression from informal, reactive responses to approaches that are agile and risk-informed. During the Tier selection process, an organization should consider its current risk management practices, threat environment, legal and regulatory requirements, business/mission objectives, and organizational constraints.

- A *Framework Profile* ("Profile") represents the outcomes based on business needs that an organization has selected from the Framework Categories and Subcategories. The Profile can be characterized as the alignment of standards, guidelines, and practices to the Framework Core in a particular implementation scenario. Profiles can be used to identify opportunities for improving cybersecurity posture by comparing a "Current" Profile (the "as is" state) with a "Target" Profile (the "to be" state). To develop a Profile, an organization can review all of the Categories and Subcategories and, based on business drivers and a risk assessment, determine which are most important; they can add Categories and Subcategories as needed to address the organization's risks. The Current Profile can then be used to support prioritization and measurement of progress toward the Target Profile, while factoring in other business needs including cost-effectiveness and innovation. Profiles can be used to conduct self-assessments and communicate within an organization or between organizations.

1.2   Risk Management and the Cybersecurity Framework

Risk management is the ongoing process of identifying, assessing, and responding to risk. To manage risk, organizations should understand the likelihood that an event will occur and the resulting impact. With this information, organizations can determine the acceptable level of risk for delivery of services and can express this as their risk tolerance.

With an understanding of risk tolerance, organizations can prioritize cybersecurity activities, enabling organizations to make informed decisions about cybersecurity expenditures. Implementation of risk management programs offers organizations the ability to quantify and communicate adjustments to their cybersecurity programs. Organizations may choose to handle risk in different ways, including mitigating the risk, transferring the risk, avoiding the risk, or accepting the risk, depending on the potential impact to the delivery of critical services.

The Framework uses risk management processes to enable organizations to inform and prioritize decisions regarding cybersecurity. It supports recurring risk assessments and validation of business drivers to help organizations select target states for cybersecurity activities that reflect desired outcomes. Thus, the Framework gives organizations the ability to dynamically select and direct improvement in cybersecurity risk management for the IT and ICS environments.

The Framework is adaptive to provide a flexible and risk-based implementation that can be used with a broad array of cybersecurity risk management processes. Examples of cybersecurity risk management processes include International Organization for Standardization (ISO) 31000:2009[3], ISO/IEC 27005:2011[4], National Institute of Standards and Technology (NIST) Special Publication (SP) 800-39[5], and the *Electricity Subsector Cybersecurity Risk Management Process* (RMP) guideline[6].

1.3   Document Overview

The remainder of this document contains the following sections and appendices:

- Section 2 describes the Framework components: the Framework Core, the Tiers, and the Profiles.
- Section 3 presents examples of how the Framework can be used.
- Appendix A presents the Framework Core in a tabular format: the Functions, Categories, Subcategories, and Informative References.
- Appendix B contains a glossary of selected terms.
- Appendix C lists acronyms used in this document.

---

[3] International Organization for Standardization, *Risk management – Principles and guidelines*, ISO 31000:2009, 2009. http://www.iso.org/iso/home/standards/iso31000.htm

[4] International Organization for Standardization/International Electrotechnical Commission, *Information technology – Security techniques – Information security risk management*, ISO/IEC 27005:2011, 2011. http://www.iso.org/iso/catalogue_detail?csnumber=56742

[5] Joint Task Force Transformation Initiative, *Managing Information Security Risk: Organization, Mission, and Information System View*, NIST Special Publication 800-39, March 2011. http://csrc.nist.gov/publications/nistpubs/800-39/SP800-39-final.pdf

[6] U.S. Department of Energy, *Electricity Subsector Cybersecurity Risk Management Process*, DOE/OE-0003, May 2012. http://energy.gov/sites/prod/files/Cybersecurity%20Risk%20Management%20Process%20Guideline%20-%20Final%20-%20May%202012.pdf

2.0   Framework Basics

The Framework provides a common language for understanding, managing, and expressing cybersecurity risk both internally and externally. It can be used to help identify and prioritize actions for reducing cybersecurity risk, and it is a tool for aligning policy, business, and technological approaches to managing that risk. It can be used to manage cybersecurity risk across entire organizations or it can be focused on the delivery of critical services within an organization. Different types of entities – including sector coordinating structures, associations, and organizations – can use the Framework for different purposes, including the creation of common Profiles.

2.1   Framework Core

The *Framework Core* provides a set of activities to achieve specific cybersecurity outcomes, and references examples of guidance to achieve those outcomes. The Core is not a checklist of actions to perform. It presents key cybersecurity outcomes identified by industry as helpful in managing cybersecurity risk. The Core comprises four elements: Functions, Categories, Subcategories, and Informative References, depicted in **Figure 1**:

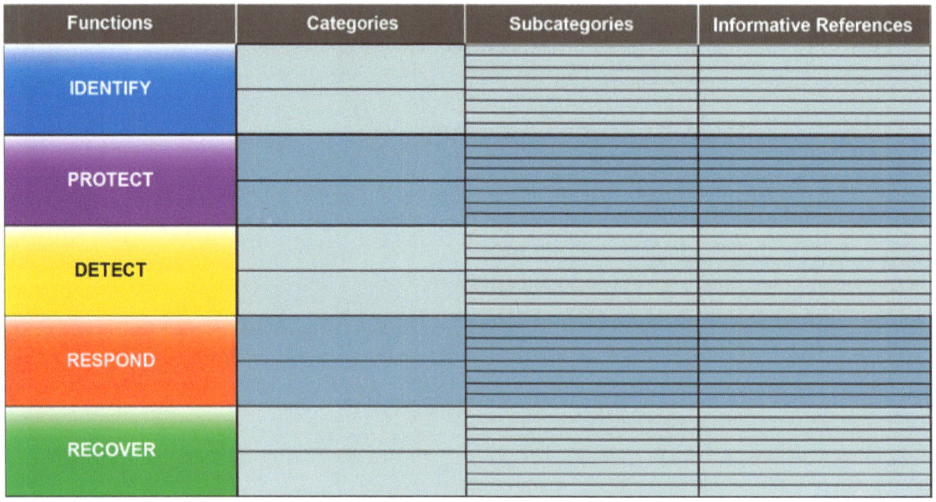

Figure 1: Framework Core Structure

The Framework Core elements work together as follows:

- **Functions** organize basic cybersecurity activities at their highest level. These Functions are Identify, Protect, Detect, Respond, and Recover. They aid an organization in expressing its management of cybersecurity risk by organizing information, enabling risk management decisions, addressing threats, and improving by learning from previous activities. The Functions also align with existing methodologies for incident management and help show the impact of investments in cybersecurity. For example, investments in planning and exercises support timely response and recovery actions, resulting in reduced impact to the delivery of services.

- **Categories** are the subdivisions of a Function into groups of cybersecurity outcomes closely tied to programmatic needs and particular activities. Examples of Categories include "Asset Management," "Access Control," and "Detection Processes."

- **Subcategories** further divide a Category into specific outcomes of technical and/or management activities. They provide a set of results that, while not exhaustive, help support achievement of the outcomes in each Category. Examples of Subcategories include "External information systems are catalogued," "Data-at-rest is protected," and "Notifications from detection systems are investigated."

- **Informative References** are specific sections of standards, guidelines, and practices common among critical infrastructure sectors that illustrate a method to achieve the outcomes associated with each Subcategory. The Informative References presented in the Framework Core are illustrative and not exhaustive. They are based upon cross-sector guidance most frequently referenced during the Framework development process.[7]

The five Framework Core Functions are defined below. These Functions are not intended to form a serial path, or lead to a static desired end state. Rather, the Functions can be performed concurrently and continuously to form an operational culture that addresses the dynamic cybersecurity risk. See Appendix A for the complete Framework Core listing.

- **Identify** – Develop the organizational understanding to manage cybersecurity risk to systems, assets, data, and capabilities.

  The activities in the Identify Function are foundational for effective use of the Framework. Understanding the business context, the resources that support critical functions, and the related cybersecurity risks enables an organization to focus and prioritize its efforts, consistent with its risk management strategy and business needs. Examples of outcome Categories within this Function include: Asset Management; Business Environment; Governance; Risk Assessment; and Risk Management Strategy.

- **Protect** – Develop and implement the appropriate safeguards to ensure delivery of critical infrastructure services.

  The Protect Function supports the ability to limit or contain the impact of a potential cybersecurity event. Examples of outcome Categories within this Function include: Access Control; Awareness and Training; Data Security; Information Protection Processes and Procedures; Maintenance; and Protective Technology.

- **Detect** – Develop and implement the appropriate activities to identify the occurrence of a cybersecurity event.

  The Detect Function enables timely discovery of cybersecurity events. Examples of outcome Categories within this Function include: Anomalies and Events; Security Continuous Monitoring; and Detection Processes.

- **Respond** – Develop and implement the appropriate activities to take action regarding a detected cybersecurity event.

---

[7] NIST developed a Compendium of informative references gathered from the Request for Information (RFI) input, Cybersecurity Framework workshops, and stakeholder engagement during the Framework development process. The Compendium includes standards, guidelines, and practices to assist with implementation. The Compendium is not intended to be an exhaustive list, but rather a starting point based on initial stakeholder input. The Compendium and other supporting material can be found at http://www.nist.gov/cyberframework/.

The Respond Function supports the ability to contain the impact of a potential cybersecurity event. Examples of outcome Categories within this Function include: Response Planning; Communications; Analysis; Mitigation; and Improvements.

- **Recover** – Develop and implement the appropriate activities to maintain plans for resilience and to restore any capabilities or services that were impaired due to a cybersecurity event.

The Recover Function supports timely recovery to normal operations to reduce the impact from a cybersecurity event. Examples of outcome Categories within this Function include: Recovery Planning; Improvements; and Communications.

2.2   Framework Implementation Tiers

The Framework Implementation Tiers ("Tiers") provide context on how an organization views cybersecurity risk and the processes in place to manage that risk. The Tiers range from Partial (Tier 1) to Adaptive (Tier 4) and describe an increasing degree of rigor and sophistication in cybersecurity risk management practices and the extent to which cybersecurity risk management is informed by business needs and is integrated into an organization's overall risk management practices. Risk management considerations include many aspects of cybersecurity, including the degree to which privacy and civil liberties considerations are integrated into an organization's management of cybersecurity risk and potential risk responses.

The Tier selection process considers an organization's current risk management practices, threat environment, legal and regulatory requirements, business/mission objectives, and organizational constraints. Organizations should determine the desired Tier, ensuring that the selected level meets the organizational goals, is feasible to implement, and reduces cybersecurity risk to critical assets and resources to levels acceptable to the organization. Organizations should consider leveraging external guidance obtained from Federal government departments and agencies, Information Sharing and Analysis Centers (ISACs), existing maturity models, or other sources to assist in determining their desired tier.

While organizations identified as Tier 1 (Partial) are encouraged to consider moving toward Tier 2 or greater, Tiers do not represent maturity levels. Progression to higher Tiers is encouraged when such a change would reduce cybersecurity risk and be cost effective. Successful implementation of the Framework is based upon achievement of the outcomes described in the organization's Target Profile(s) and not upon Tier determination.

The Tier definitions are as follows:

Tier 1: Partial

- *Risk Management Process* – Organizational cybersecurity risk management practices are not formalized, and risk is managed in an *ad hoc* and sometimes reactive manner. Prioritization of cybersecurity activities may not be directly informed by organizational risk objectives, the threat environment, or business/mission requirements.

- *Integrated Risk Management Program* – There is limited awareness of cybersecurity risk at the organizational level and an organization-wide approach to managing cybersecurity risk has not been established. The organization implements cybersecurity risk management on an irregular, case-by-case basis due to varied experience or information gained from outside sources. The organization may not have processes that enable cybersecurity information to be shared within the organization.

- *External Participation* – An organization may not have the processes in place to participate in coordination or collaboration with other entities.

Tier 2: Risk Informed

- *Risk Management Process* – Risk management practices are approved by management but may not be established as organizational-wide policy. Prioritization of cybersecurity activities is directly informed by organizational risk objectives, the threat environment, or business/mission requirements.

- *Integrated Risk Management Program* – There is an awareness of cybersecurity risk at the organizational level but an organization-wide approach to managing cybersecurity risk has not been established. Risk-informed, management-approved processes and procedures are defined and implemented, and staff has adequate resources to perform their cybersecurity duties. Cybersecurity information is shared within the organization on an informal basis.

- *External Participation* – The organization knows its role in the larger ecosystem, but has not formalized its capabilities to interact and share information externally.

Tier 3: Repeatable

- *Risk Management Process* – The organization's risk management practices are formally approved and expressed as policy. Organizational cybersecurity practices are regularly updated based on the application of risk management processes to changes in business/mission requirements and a changing threat and technology landscape.

- *Integrated Risk Management Program* – There is an organization-wide approach to manage cybersecurity risk. Risk-informed policies, processes, and procedures are defined, implemented as intended, and reviewed. Consistent methods are in place to respond effectively to changes in risk. Personnel possess the knowledge and skills to perform their appointed roles and responsibilities.

- *External Participation* – The organization understands its dependencies and partners and receives information from these partners that enables collaboration and risk-based management decisions within the organization in response to events.

Tier 4: Adaptive

- *Risk Management Process* – The organization adapts its cybersecurity practices based on lessons learned and predictive indicators derived from previous and current cybersecurity activities. Through a process of continuous improvement incorporating advanced cybersecurity technologies and practices, the organization actively adapts to a changing cybersecurity landscape and responds to evolving and sophisticated threats in a timely manner.

- *Integrated Risk Management Program* – There is an organization-wide approach to managing cybersecurity risk that uses risk-informed policies, processes, and procedures to address potential cybersecurity events. Cybersecurity risk management is part of the organizational culture and evolves from an awareness of previous activities, information shared by other sources, and continuous awareness of activities on their systems and networks.

- *External Participation* – The organization manages risk and actively shares information with partners to ensure that accurate, current information is being distributed and consumed to improve cybersecurity before a cybersecurity event occurs.

2.3   Framework Profile

The Framework Profile ("Profile") is the alignment of the Functions, Categories, and Subcategories with the business requirements, risk tolerance, and resources of the organization. A Profile enables organizations to establish a roadmap for reducing cybersecurity risk that is well aligned with organizational and sector goals, considers legal/regulatory requirements and industry best practices, and reflects risk management priorities. Given the complexity of many organizations, they may choose to have multiple profiles, aligned with particular components and recognizing their individual needs.

Framework Profiles can be used to describe the current state or the desired target state of specific cybersecurity activities. The Current Profile indicates the cybersecurity outcomes that are currently being achieved. The Target Profile indicates the outcomes needed to achieve the desired cybersecurity risk management goals. Profiles support business/mission requirements and aid in the communication of risk within and between organizations. This Framework document does not prescribe Profile templates, allowing for flexibility in implementation.

Comparison of Profiles (e.g., the Current Profile and Target Profile) may reveal gaps to be addressed to meet cybersecurity risk management objectives. An action plan to address these gaps can contribute to the roadmap described above. Prioritization of gap mitigation is driven by the organization's business needs and risk management processes. This risk-based approach enables an organization to gauge resource estimates (e.g., staffing, funding) to achieve cybersecurity goals in a cost-effective, prioritized manner.

2.4   Coordination of Framework Implementation

Figure 2 describes a common flow of information and decisions at the following levels within an organization:

- Executive
- Business/Process
- Implementation/Operations

The executive level communicates the mission priorities, available resources, and overall risk tolerance to the business/process level. The business/process level uses the information as inputs into the risk management process, and then collaborates with the implementation/operations level to communicate business needs and create a Profile. The implementation/operations level communicates the Profile implementation progress to the business/process level. The business/process level uses this information to perform an impact assessment. Business/process level management reports the outcomes of that impact assessment to the executive level to inform the organization's overall risk management process and to the implementation/operations level for awareness of business impact.

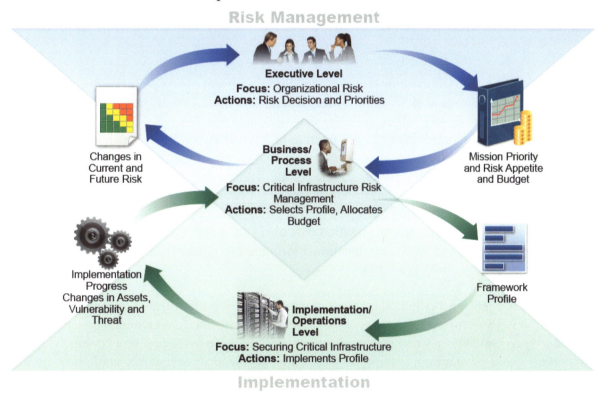

Figure 2: Notional Information and Decision Flows within an Organization

3.0 How to Use the Framework

An organization can use the Framework as a key part of its systematic process for identifying, assessing, and managing cybersecurity risk. The Framework is not designed to replace existing processes; an organization can use its current process and overlay it onto the Framework to determine gaps in its current cybersecurity risk approach and develop a roadmap to improvement. Utilizing the Framework as a cybersecurity risk management tool, an organization can determine activities that are most important to critical service delivery and prioritize expenditures to maximize the impact of the investment.

The Framework is designed to complement existing business and cybersecurity operations. It can serve as the foundation for a new cybersecurity program or a mechanism for improving an existing program. The Framework provides a means of expressing cybersecurity requirements to business partners and customers and can help identify gaps in an organization's cybersecurity practices. It also provides a general set of considerations and processes for considering privacy and civil liberties implications in the context of a cybersecurity program.

The following sections present different ways in which organizations can use the Framework.

3.1 Basic Review of Cybersecurity Practices

The Framework can be used to compare an organization's current cybersecurity activities with those outlined in the Framework Core. Through the creation of a Current Profile, organizations can examine the extent to which they are achieving the outcomes described in the Core Categories and Subcategories, aligned with the five high-level Functions: Identify, Protect, Detect, Respond, and Recover. An organization may find that it is already achieving the desired outcomes, thus managing cybersecurity commensurate with the known risk. Conversely, an organization may determine that it has opportunities to (or needs to) improve. The organization can use that information to develop an action plan to strengthen existing cybersecurity practices and reduce cybersecurity risk. An organization may also find that it is overinvesting to achieve certain outcomes. The organization can use this information to reprioritize resources to strengthen other cybersecurity practices.

While they do not replace a risk management process, these five high-level Functions will provide a concise way for senior executives and others to distill the fundamental concepts of cybersecurity risk so that they can assess how identified risks are managed, and how their organization stacks up at a high level against existing cybersecurity standards, guidelines, and practices. The Framework can also help an organization answer fundamental questions, including "How are we doing?" Then they can move in a more informed way to strengthen their cybersecurity practices where and when deemed necessary.

3.2 Establishing or Improving a Cybersecurity Program

The following steps illustrate how an organization could use the Framework to create a new cybersecurity program or improve an existing program. These steps should be repeated as necessary to continuously improve cybersecurity.

Step 1: Prioritize and Scope. The organization identifies its business/mission objectives and high-level organizational priorities. With this information, the organization makes strategic decisions regarding cybersecurity implementations and determines the scope of systems and assets that support the selected business line or process. The Framework can be adapted to support the different business lines or processes within an organization, which may have different business needs and associated risk tolerance.

Step 2: Orient. Once the scope of the cybersecurity program has been determined for the business line or process, the organization identifies related systems and assets, regulatory requirements, and overall risk approach. The organization then identifies threats to, and vulnerabilities of, those systems and assets.

Step 3: Create a Current Profile. The organization develops a Current Profile by indicating which Category and Subcategory outcomes from the Framework Core are currently being achieved.

Step 4: Conduct a Risk Assessment. This assessment could be guided by the organization's overall risk management process or previous risk assessment activities. The organization analyzes the operational environment in order to discern the likelihood of a cybersecurity event and the impact that the event could have on the organization. It is important that organizations seek to incorporate emerging risks and threat and vulnerability data to facilitate a robust understanding of the likelihood and impact of cybersecurity events.

Step 5: Create a Target Profile. The organization creates a Target Profile that focuses on the assessment of the Framework Categories and Subcategories describing the organization's desired cybersecurity outcomes. Organizations also may develop their own additional Categories and Subcategories to account for unique organizational risks. The organization may also consider influences and requirements of external stakeholders such as sector entities, customers, and business partners when creating a Target Profile.

Step 6: Determine, Analyze, and Prioritize Gaps. The organization compares the Current Profile and the Target Profile to determine gaps. Next it creates a prioritized action plan to address those gaps that draws upon mission drivers, a cost/benefit analysis, and understanding of risk to achieve the outcomes in the Target Profile. The organization then determines resources necessary to address the gaps. Using Profiles in this manner enables the organization to make informed decisions about cybersecurity activities, supports risk management, and enables the organization to perform cost-effective, targeted improvements.

Step 7: Implement Action Plan. The organization determines which actions to take in regards to the gaps, if any, identified in the previous step. It then monitors its current cybersecurity practices against the Target Profile. For further guidance, the Framework identifies example Informative References regarding the Categories and Subcategories, but organizations should determine which standards, guidelines, and practices, including those that are sector specific, work best for their needs.

An organization may repeat the steps as needed to continuously assess and improve its cybersecurity. For instance, organizations may find that more frequent repetition of the orient step improves the quality of risk assessments. Furthermore, organizations may monitor progress through iterative updates to the Current Profile, subsequently comparing the Current Profile to the Target Profile. Organizations may also utilize this process to align their cybersecurity program with their desired Framework Implementation Tier.

3.3   Communicating Cybersecurity Requirements with Stakeholders

The Framework provides a common language to communicate requirements among interdependent stakeholders responsible for the delivery of essential critical infrastructure services. Examples include:

- An organization may utilize a Target Profile to express cybersecurity risk management requirements to an external service provider (e.g., a cloud provider to which it is exporting data).
- An organization may express its cybersecurity state through a Current Profile to report results or to compare with acquisition requirements.
- A critical infrastructure owner/operator, having identified an external partner on whom that infrastructure depends, may use a Target Profile to convey required Categories and Subcategories.
- A critical infrastructure sector may establish a Target Profile that can be used among its constituents as an initial baseline Profile to build their tailored Target Profiles.

3.4   Identifying Opportunities for New or Revised Informative References

The Framework can be used to identify opportunities for new or revised standards, guidelines, or practices where additional Informative References would help organizations address emerging needs. An organization implementing a given Subcategory, or developing a new Subcategory, might discover that there are few Informative References, if any, for a related activity. To address that need, the organization might collaborate with technology leaders and/or standards bodies to draft, develop, and coordinate standards, guidelines, or practices.

3.5   Methodology to Protect Privacy and Civil Liberties

This section describes a methodology as required by the Executive Order to address individual privacy and civil liberties implications that may result from cybersecurity operations. This methodology is intended to be a general set of considerations and processes since privacy and civil liberties implications may differ by sector or over time and organizations may address these considerations and processes with a range of technical implementations. Nonetheless, not all activities in a cybersecurity program may give rise to these considerations. Consistent with Section 3.4, technical privacy standards, guidelines, and additional best practices may need to be developed to support improved technical implementations.

Privacy and civil liberties implications may arise when personal information is used, collected, processed, maintained, or disclosed in connection with an organization's cybersecurity activities. Some examples of activities that bear privacy or civil liberties considerations may include: cybersecurity activities that result in the over-collection or over-retention of personal information; disclosure or use of personal information unrelated to cybersecurity activities; cybersecurity mitigation activities that result in denial of service or other similar potentially adverse impacts, including activities such as some types of incident detection or monitoring that may impact freedom of expression or association.

The government and agents of the government have a direct responsibility to protect civil liberties arising from cybersecurity activities. As referenced in the methodology below, government or agents of the government that own or operate critical infrastructure should have a process in place to support compliance of cybersecurity activities with applicable privacy laws, regulations, and Constitutional requirements.

To address privacy implications, organizations may consider how, in circumstances where such measures are appropriate, their cybersecurity program might incorporate privacy principles such as: data minimization in the collection, disclosure, and retention of personal information material related to the cybersecurity incident; use limitations outside of cybersecurity activities on any information collected specifically for cybersecurity activities; transparency for certain cybersecurity activities; individual consent and redress for adverse impacts arising from use of personal information in cybersecurity activities; data quality, integrity, and security; and accountability and auditing.

As organizations assess the Framework Core in Appendix A, the following processes and activities may be considered as a means to address the above-referenced privacy and civil liberties implications:

Governance of cybersecurity risk

- An organization's assessment of cybersecurity risk and potential risk responses considers the privacy implications of its cybersecurity program
- Individuals with cybersecurity-related privacy responsibilities report to appropriate management and are appropriately trained
- Process is in place to support compliance of cybersecurity activities with applicable privacy laws, regulations, and Constitutional requirements
- Process is in place to assess implementation of the foregoing organizational measures and controls

Approaches to identifying and authorizing individuals to access organizational assets and systems

- Steps are taken to identify and address the privacy implications of access control measures to the extent that they involve collection, disclosure, or use of personal information

Awareness and training measures

- Applicable information from organizational privacy policies is included in cybersecurity workforce training and awareness activities
- Service providers that provide cybersecurity-related services for the organization are informed about the organization's applicable privacy policies

Anomalous activity detection and system and assets monitoring

- Process is in place to conduct a privacy review of an organization's anomalous activity detection and cybersecurity monitoring

Response activities, including information sharing or other mitigation efforts

- Process is in place to assess and address whether, when, how, and the extent to which personal information is shared outside the organization as part of cybersecurity information sharing activities
- Process is in place to conduct a privacy review of an organization's cybersecurity mitigation efforts

Appendix A: Framework Core

This appendix presents the Framework Core: a listing of Functions, Categories, Subcategories, and Informative References that describe specific cybersecurity activities that are common across all critical infrastructure sectors. The chosen presentation format for the Framework Core does not suggest a specific implementation order or imply a degree of importance of the Categories, Subcategories, and Informative References. The Framework Core presented in this appendix represents a common set of activities for managing cybersecurity risk. While the Framework is not exhaustive, it is extensible, allowing organizations, sectors, and other entities to use Subcategories and Informative References that are cost-effective and efficient and that enable them to manage their cybersecurity risk. Activities can be selected from the Framework Core during the Profile creation process and additional Categories, Subcategories, and Informative References may be added to the Profile. An organization's risk management processes, legal/regulatory requirements, business/mission objectives, and organizational constraints guide the selection of these activities during Profile creation. Personal information is considered a component of data or assets referenced in the Categories when assessing security risks and protections.

While the intended outcomes identified in the Functions, Categories, and Subcategories are the same for IT and ICS, the operational environments and considerations for IT and ICS differ. ICS have a direct effect on the physical world, including potential risks to the health and safety of individuals, and impact on the environment. Additionally, ICS have unique performance and reliability requirements compared with IT, and the goals of safety and efficiency must be considered when implementing cybersecurity measures.

For ease of use, each component of the Framework Core is given a unique identifier. Functions and Categories each have a unique alphabetic identifier, as shown in Table 1. Subcategories within each Category are referenced numerically; the unique identifier for each Subcategory is included in Table 2.

Additional supporting material relating to the Framework can be found on the NIST website at http://www.nist.gov/cyberframework/.

Table 1: Function and Category Unique Identifiers

Function Unique Identifier	Function	Category Unique Identifier	Category
ID	Identify	ID.AM	Asset Management
		ID.BE	Business Environment
		ID.GV	Governance
		ID.RA	Risk Assessment
		ID.RM	Risk Management Strategy
PR	Protect	PR.AC	Access Control
		PR.AT	Awareness and Training
		PR.DS	Data Security
		PR.IP	Information Protection Processes and Procedures
		PR.MA	Maintenance
		PR.PT	Protective Technology
DE	Detect	DE.AE	Anomalies and Events
		DE.CM	Security Continuous Monitoring
		DE.DP	Detection Processes
RS	Respond	RS.RP	Response Planning
		RS.CO	Communications
		RS.AN	Analysis
		RS.MI	Mitigation
		RS.IM	Improvements
RC	Recover	RC.RP	Recovery Planning
		RC.IM	Improvements
		RC.CO	Communications

Table 2: Framework Core

Function	Category	Subcategory	Informative References
IDENTIFY (ID)	**Asset Management (ID.AM):** The data, personnel, devices, systems, and facilities that enable the organization to achieve business purposes are identified and managed consistent with their relative importance to business objectives and the organization's risk strategy.	**ID.AM-1:** Physical devices and systems within the organization are inventoried	• CCS CSC 1 • COBIT 5 BAI09.01, BAI09.02 • ISA 62443-2-1:2009 4.2.3.4 • ISA 62443-3-3:2013 SR 7.8 • ISO/IEC 27001:2013 A.8.1.1, A.8.1.2 • NIST SP 800-53 Rev. 4 CM-8
		ID.AM-2: Software platforms and applications within the organization are inventoried	• CCS CSC 2 • COBIT 5 BAI09.01, BAI09.02, BAI09.05 • ISA 62443-2-1:2009 4.2.3.4 • ISA 62443-3-3:2013 SR 7.8 • ISO/IEC 27001:2013 A.8.1.1, A.8.1.2 • NIST SP 800-53 Rev. 4 CM-8
		ID.AM-3: Organizational communication and data flows are mapped	• CCS CSC 1 • COBIT 5 DSS05.02 • ISA 62443-2-1:2009 4.2.3.4 • ISO/IEC 27001:2013 A.13.2.1 • NIST SP 800-53 Rev. 4 AC-4, CA-3, CA-9, PL-8
		ID.AM-4: External information systems are catalogued	• COBIT 5 APO02.02 • ISO/IEC 27001:2013 A.11.2.6 • NIST SP 800-53 Rev. 4 AC-20, SA-9
		ID.AM-5: Resources (e.g., hardware, devices, data, and software) are prioritized based on their classification, criticality, and business value	• COBIT 5 APO03.03, APO03.04, BAI09.02 • ISA 62443-2-1:2009 4.2.3.6 • ISO/IEC 27001:2013 A.8.2.1 • NIST SP 800-53 Rev. 4 CP-2, RA-2, SA-14
		ID.AM-6: Cybersecurity roles and responsibilities for the entire workforce and third-party stakeholders (e.g., suppliers, customers, partners) are established	• COBIT 5 APO01.02, DSS06.03 • ISA 62443-2-1:2009 4.3.2.3.3 • ISO/IEC 27001:2013 A.6.1.1

Function	Category	Subcategory	Informative References
			• NIST SP 800-53 Rev. 4 CP-2, PS-7, PM-11
	Business Environment (ID.BE): The organization's mission, objectives, stakeholders, and activities are understood and prioritized; this information is used to inform cybersecurity roles, responsibilities, and risk management decisions.	**ID.BE-1:** The organization's role in the supply chain is identified and communicated	• COBIT 5 APO08.04, APO08.05, APO10.03, APO10.04, APO10.05 • ISO/IEC 27001:2013 A.15.1.3, A.15.2.1, A.15.2.2 • NIST SP 800-53 Rev. 4 CP-2, SA-12
		ID.BE-2: The organization's place in critical infrastructure and its industry sector is identified and communicated	• COBIT 5 APO02.06, APO03.01 • NIST SP 800-53 Rev. 4 PM-8
		ID.BE-3: Priorities for organizational mission, objectives, and activities are established and communicated	• COBIT 5 APO02.01, APO02.06, APO03.01 • ISA 62443-2-1:2009 4.2.2.1, 4.2.3.6 • NIST SP 800-53 Rev. 4 PM-11, SA-14
		ID.BE-4: Dependencies and critical functions for delivery of critical services are established	• ISO/IEC 27001:2013 A.11.2.2, A.11.2.3, A.12.1.3 • NIST SP 800-53 Rev. 4 CP-8, PE-9, PE-11, PM-8, SA-14
		ID.BE-5: Resilience requirements to support delivery of critical services are established	• COBIT 5 DSS04.02 • ISO/IEC 27001:2013 A.11.1.4, A.17.1.1, A.17.1.2, A.17.2.1 • NIST SP 800-53 Rev. 4 CP-2, CP-11, SA-14
	Governance (ID.GV): The policies, procedures, and processes to manage and monitor the organization's regulatory, legal, risk, environmental, and operational requirements are understood and inform the management of cybersecurity risk.	**ID.GV-1:** Organizational information security policy is established	• COBIT 5 APO01.03, EDM01.01, EDM01.02 • ISA 62443-2-1:2009 4.3.2.6 • ISO/IEC 27001:2013 A.5.1.1 • NIST SP 800-53 Rev. 4 -1 controls from all families
		ID.GV-2: Information security roles & responsibilities are coordinated and aligned with internal roles and external partners	• COBIT 5 APO13.12 • ISA 62443-2-1:2009 4.3.2.3.3 • ISO/IEC 27001:2013 A.6.1.1, A.7.2.1 • NIST SP 800-53 Rev. 4 PM-1, PS-7
		ID.GV-3: Legal and regulatory requirements regarding cybersecurity,	• COBIT 5 MEA03.01, MEA03.04 • ISA 62443-2-1:2009 4.4.3.7

Function	Category	Subcategory	Informative References
		including privacy and civil liberties obligations, are understood and managed	• **ISO/IEC 27001:2013** A.18.1 • **NIST SP 800-53 Rev. 4** - l controls from all families (except PM-1)
		ID.GV-4: Governance and risk management processes address cybersecurity risks	• **COBIT 5** DSS04.02 • **ISA 62443-2-1:2009** 4.2.3.1, 4.2.3.3, 4.2.3.8, 4.2.3.9, 4.2.3.11, 4.3.2.4.3, 4.3.2.6.3 • **NIST SP 800-53 Rev. 4** PM-9, PM-11
	Risk Assessment (ID.RA): The organization understands the cybersecurity risk to organizational operations (including mission, functions, image, or reputation), organizational assets, and individuals.	**ID.RA-1**: Asset vulnerabilities are identified and documented	• **CCS CSC** 4 • **COBIT 5** APO12.01, APO12.02, APO12.03, APO12.04 • **ISA 62443-2-1:2009** 4.2.3, 4.2.3.7, 4.2.3.9, 4.2.3.12 • **ISO/IEC 27001:2013** A.12.6.1, A.18.2.3 • **NIST SP 800-53 Rev. 4** CA-2, CA-7, CA-8, RA-3, RA-5, SA-5, SA-11, SI-2, SI-4, SI-5
		ID.RA-2: Threat and vulnerability information is received from information sharing forums and sources	• **ISA 62443-2-1:2009** 4.2.3, 4.2.3.9, 4.2.3.12 • **ISO/IEC 27001:2013** A.6.1.4 • **NIST SP 800-53 Rev. 4** PM-15, PM-16, SI-5
		ID.RA-3: Threats, both internal and external, are identified and documented	• **COBIT 5** APO12.01, APO12.02, APO12.03, APO12.04 • **ISA 62443-2-1:2009** 4.2.3, 4.2.3.9, 4.2.3.12 • **NIST SP 800-53 Rev. 4** RA-3, SI-5, PM-12, PM-16
		ID.RA-4: Potential business impacts and likelihoods are identified	• **COBIT 5** DSS04.02 • **ISA 62443-2-1:2009** 4.2.3, 4.2.3.9, 4.2.3.12 • **NIST SP 800-53 Rev. 4** RA-2, RA-3, PM-9, PM-11, SA-14
		ID.RA-5: Threats, vulnerabilities, likelihoods, and impacts are used to determine risk	• **COBIT 5** APO12.02 • **ISO/IEC 27001:2013** A.12.6.1 • **NIST SP 800-53 Rev. 4** RA-2, RA-3, PM-16
		ID.RA-6: Risk responses are identified and	• **COBIT 5** APO12.05, APO13.02

Function	Category	Subcategory	Informative References
		prioritized	• **NIST SP 800-53 Rev. 4** PM-4, PM-9
	Risk Management Strategy (ID.RM): The organization's priorities, constraints, risk tolerances, and assumptions are established and used to support operational risk decisions.	**ID.RM-1:** Risk management processes are established, managed, and agreed to by organizational stakeholders	• **COBIT 5** APO12.04, APO12.05, APO13.02, BAI02.03, BAI04.02 • **ISA 62443-2-1:2009** 4.3.4.2 • **NIST SP 800-53 Rev. 4** PM-9
		ID.RM-2: Organizational risk tolerance is determined and clearly expressed	• **COBIT 5** APO12.06 • **ISA 62443-2-1:2009** 4.3.2.6.5 • **NIST SP 800-53 Rev. 4** PM-9
		ID.RM-3: The organization's determination of risk tolerance is informed by its role in critical infrastructure and sector specific risk analysis	• **NIST SP 800-53 Rev. 4** PM-8, PM-9, PM-11, SA-14
PROTECT (PR)	**Access Control (PR.AC):** Access to assets and associated facilities is limited to authorized users, processes, or devices, and to authorized activities and transactions.	**PR.AC-1:** Identities and credentials are managed for authorized devices and users	• CCS CSC 16 • **COBIT 5** DSS05.04, DSS06.03 • **ISA 62443-2-1:2009** 4.3.3.5.1 • **ISA 62443-3-3:2013** SR 1.1, SR 1.2, SR 1.3, SR 1.4, SR 1.5, SR 1.7, SR 1.8, SR 1.9 • **ISO/IEC 27001:2013** A.9.2.1, A.9.2.2, A.9.2.4, A.9.3.1, A.9.4.2, A.9.4.3 • **NIST SP 800-53 Rev. 4** AC-2, IA Family
		PR.AC-2: Physical access to assets is managed and protected	• **COBIT 5** DSS01.04, DSS05.05 • **ISA 62443-2-1:2009** 4.3.3.3.2, 4.3.3.3.8 • **ISO/IEC 27001:2013** A.11.1.1, A.11.1.2, A.11.1.4, A.11.1.6, A.11.2.3 • **NIST SP 800-53 Rev. 4** PE-2, PE-3, PE-4, PE-5, PE-6, PE-9
		PR.AC-3: Remote access is managed	• **COBIT 5** APO13.01, DSS01.04, DSS05.03 • **ISA 62443-2-1:2009** 4.3.3.6.6 • **ISA 62443-3-3:2013** SR 1.13, SR 2.6 • **ISO/IEC 27001:2013** A.6.2.2, A.13.1.1, A.13.2.1

Function	Category	Subcategory	Informative References
		PR.AC-4: Access permissions are managed, incorporating the principles of least privilege and separation of duties	• **CCS CSC** 12, 15 • **ISA 62443-2-1:2009** 4.3.3.7.3 • **ISA 62443-3-3:2013** SR 2.1 • **ISO/IEC 27001:2013** A.6.1.2, A.9.1.2, A.9.2.3, A.9.4.1, A.9.4.4 • **NIST SP 800-53 Rev. 4** AC-2, AC-3, AC-5, AC-6, AC-16
		PR.AC-5: Network integrity is protected, incorporating network segregation where appropriate	• **ISA 62443-2-1:2009** 4.3.3.4 • **ISA 62443-3-3:2013** SR 3.1, SR 3.8 • **ISO/IEC 27001:2013** A.13.1.1, A.13.1.3, A.13.2.1 • **NIST SP 800-53 Rev. 4** AC-4, SC-7
	Awareness and Training (PR.AT): The organization's personnel and partners are provided cybersecurity awareness education and are adequately trained to perform their information security-related duties and responsibilities consistent with related policies, procedures, and agreements.	**PR.AT-1:** All users are informed and trained	• **CCS CSC** 9 • **COBIT 5** APO07.03, BAI05.07 • **ISA 62443-2-1:2009** 4.3.2.4.2 • **ISO/IEC 27001:2013** A.7.2.2 • **NIST SP 800-53 Rev. 4** AT-2, PM-13
		PR.AT-2: Privileged users understand roles & responsibilities	• **CCS CSC** 9 • **COBIT 5** APO07.02, DSS06.03 • **ISA 62443-2-1:2009** 4.3.2.4.2, 4.3.2.4.3 • **ISO/IEC 27001:2013** A.6.1.1, A.7.2.2 • **NIST SP 800-53 Rev. 4** AT-3, PM-13
		PR.AT-3: Third-party stakeholders (e.g., suppliers, customers, partners) understand roles & responsibilities	• **CCS CSC** 9 • **COBIT 5** APO07.03, APO10.04, APO10.05 • **ISA 62443-2-1:2009** 4.3.2.4.2 • **ISO/IEC 27001:2013** A.6.1.1, A.7.2.2 • **NIST SP 800-53 Rev. 4** PS-7, SA-9
		PR.AT-4: Senior executives understand roles & responsibilities	• **CCS CSC** 9 • **COBIT 5** APO07.03

Function	Category	Subcategory	Informative References
		PR.AT-5: Physical and information security personnel understand roles & responsibilities	• ISA 62443-2-1:2009 4.3.2.4.2 • ISO/IEC 27001:2013 A.6.1.1, A.7.2.2, • NIST SP 800-53 Rev. 4 AT-3, PM-13
			• CCS CSC 9 • COBIT 5 APO07.03 • ISA 62443-2-1:2009 4.3.2.4.2 • ISO/IEC 27001:2013 A.6.1.1, A.7.2.2, • NIST SP 800-53 Rev. 4 AT-3, PM-13
	Data Security (PR.DS): Information and records (data) are managed consistent with the organization's risk strategy to protect the confidentiality, integrity, and availability of information.	**PR.DS-1:** Data-at-rest is protected	• CCS CSC 17 • COBIT 5 APO01.06, BAI02.01, BAI06.01, DSS06.06 • ISA 62443-3-3:2013 SR 3.4, SR 4.1 • ISO/IEC 27001:2013 A.8.2.3 • NIST SP 800-53 Rev. 4 SC-28
		PR.DS-2: Data-in-transit is protected	• CCS CSC 17 • COBIT 5 APO01.06, DSS06.06 • ISA 62443-3-3:2013 SR 3.1, SR 3.8, SR 4.1, SR 4.2 • ISO/IEC 27001:2013 A.8.2.3, A.13.1.1, A.13.2.1, A.13.2.3, A.14.1.2, A.14.1.3 • NIST SP 800-53 Rev. 4 SC-8
		PR.DS-3: Assets are formally managed throughout removal, transfers, and disposition	• COBIT 5 BAI09.03 • ISA 62443-2-1:2009 4.4.3.3.9, 4.3.4.4.1 • ISA 62443-3-3:2013 SR 4.2 • ISO/IEC 27001:2013 A.8.2.3, A.8.3.1, A.8.3.2, A.8.3.3, A.11.2.7 • NIST SP 800-53 Rev. 4 CM-8, MP-6, PE-16
		PR.DS-4: Adequate capacity to ensure availability is maintained	• COBIT 5 APO13.01 • ISA 62443-3-3:2013 SR 7.1, SR 7.2 • ISO/IEC 27001:2013 A.12.3.1

Function	Category	Subcategory	Informative References
		PR.DS-5: Protections against data leaks are implemented	• **NIST SP 800-53 Rev. 4** AU-4, CP-2, SC-5 • **CCS CSC** 17 • **COBIT 5** APO01.06 • **ISA 62443-3-3:2013** SR 5.2 • **ISO/IEC 27001:2013** A.6.1.2, A.7.1.1, A.7.1.2, A.7.3.1, A.8.2.2, A.8.2.3, A.9.1.1, A.9.1.2, A.9.2.3, A.9.4.1, A.9.4.4, A.9.4.5, A.13.1.3, A.13.2.1, A.13.2.3, A.13.2.4, A.14.1.2, A.14.1.3 • **NIST SP 800-53 Rev. 4** AC-4, AC-5, AC-6, PE-19, PS-3, PS-6, SC-7, SC-8, SC-13, SC-31, SI-4
		PR.DS-6: Integrity checking mechanisms are used to verify software, firmware, and information integrity	• **ISA 62443-3-3:2013** SR 3.1, SR 3.3, SR 3.4, SR 3.8 • **ISO/IEC 27001:2013** A.12.2.1, A.12.5.1, A.14.1.2, A.14.1.3 • **NIST SP 800-53 Rev. 4** SI-7
		PR.DS-7: The development and testing environment(s) are separate from the production environment	• **COBIT 5** BAI07.04 • **ISO/IEC 27001:2013** A.12.1.4 • **NIST SP 800-53 Rev. 4** CM-2
	Information Protection Processes and Procedures (PR.IP): Security policies (that address purpose, scope, roles, responsibilities, management commitment, and coordination among organizational entities), processes, and procedures are maintained and used to manage protection of information systems and assets.	**PR.IP-1:** A baseline configuration of information technology/industrial control systems is created and maintained	• **CCS CSC** 3, 10 • **COBIT 5** BAI10.01, BAI10.02, BAI10.03, BAI10.05 • **ISA 62443-2-1:2009** 4.3.4.3.2, 4.3.4.3.3 • **ISA 62443-3-3:2013** SR 7.6 • **ISO/IEC 27001:2013** A.12.1.2, A.12.5.1, A.12.6.2, A.14.2.2, A.14.2.3, A.14.2.4 • **NIST SP 800-53 Rev. 4** CM-2, CM-3, CM-4, CM-5, CM-6, CM-7, CM-9, SA-10
		PR.IP-2: A System Development Life Cycle to manage systems is implemented	• **COBIT 5** APO13.01 • **ISA 62443-2-1:2009** 4.3.4.3.3 • **ISO/IEC 27001:2013** A.6.1.5, A.14.1.1, A.14.2.1, A.14.2.5

Function	Category	Subcategory	Informative References
			• **NIST SP 800-53 Rev. 4** SA-3, SA-4, SA-8, SA-10, SA-11, SA-12, SA-15, SA-17, PL-8
		PR.IP-3: Configuration change control processes are in place	• **COBIT 5** BAI06.01, BAI01.06 • **ISA 62443-2-1:2009** 4.3.4.3.2, 4.3.4.3.3 • **ISA 62443-3-3:2013** SR 7.6 • **ISO/IEC 27001:2013** A.12.1.2, A.12.5.1, A.12.6.2, A.14.2.2, A.14.2.3, A.14.2.4 • **NIST SP 800-53 Rev. 4** CM-3, CM-4, SA-10
		PR.IP-4: Backups of information are conducted, maintained, and tested periodically	• **COBIT 5** APO13.01 • **ISA 62443-2-1:2009** 4.3.4.3.9 • **ISA 62443-3-3:2013** SR 7.3, SR 7.4 • **ISO/IEC 27001:2013** A.12.3.1, A.17.1.2A.17.1.3, A.18.1.3 • **NIST SP 800-53 Rev. 4** CP-4, CP-6, CP-9
		PR.IP-5: Policy and regulations regarding the physical operating environment for organizational assets are met	• **COBIT 5** DSS01.04, DSS05.05 • **ISA 62443-2-1:2009** 4.3.3.3.1 4.3.3.3.2, 4.3.3.3, 4.3.3.3.5, 4.3.3.3.6 • **ISO/IEC 27001:2013** A.11.1.4, A.11.2.1, A.11.2.2, A.11.2.3 • **NIST SP 800-53 Rev. 4** PE-10, PE-12, PE-13, PE-14, PE-15, PE-18
		PR.IP-6: Data is destroyed according to policy	• **COBIT 5** BAI09.03 • **ISA 62443-2-1:2009** 4.3.4.4.4 • **ISA 62443-3-3:2013** SR 4.2 • **ISO/IEC 27001:2013** A.8.2.3, A.8.3.1, A.8.3.2, A.11.2.7 • **NIST SP 800-53 Rev. 4** MP-6
		PR.IP-7: Protection processes are continuously improved	• **COBIT 5** APO11.06, DSS04.05 • **ISA 62443-2-1:2009** 4.4.3.1, 4.4.3.2, 4.4.3.3, 4.4.3.4, 4.4.3.5, 4.4.3.6, 4.4.3.7, 4.4.3.8 • **NIST SP 800-53 Rev. 4** CA-2, CA-7, CP-2, IR-

Function	Category	Subcategory	Informative References
			• 8, PL-2, PM-6
		PR.IP-8: Effectiveness of protection technologies is shared with appropriate parties	• **ISO/IEC 27001:2013** A.16.1.6 • **NIST SP 800-53 Rev. 4** AC-21, CA-7, SI-4
		PR.IP-9: Response plans (Incident Response and Business Continuity) and recovery plans (Incident Recovery and Disaster Recovery) are in place and managed	• **COBIT 5** DSS04.03 • **ISA 62443-2-1:2009** 4.3.2.5.3, 4.3.4.5.1 • **ISO/IEC 27001:2013** A.16.1.1, A.17.1.1, A.17.1.2 • **NIST SP 800-53 Rev. 4** CP-2, IR-8
		PR.IP-10: Response and recovery plans are tested	• **ISA 62443-2-1:2009** 4.3.2.5.7, 4.3.4.5.11 • **ISA 62443-3-3:2013** SR 3.3 • **ISO/IEC 27001:2013** A.17.1.3 • **NIST SP 800-53 Rev. 4** CP-4, IR-3, PM-14
		PR.IP-11: Cybersecurity is included in human resources practices (e.g., deprovisioning, personnel screening)	• **COBIT 5** APO07.01, APO07.02, APO07.03, APO07.04, APO07.05 • **ISA 62443-2-1:2009** 4.3.3.2.1, 4.3.3.2.2, 4.3.3.2.3 • **ISO/IEC 27001:2013** A.7.1.1, A.7.3.1, A.8.1.4 • **NIST SP 800-53 Rev. 4** PS Family
		PR.IP-12: A vulnerability management plan is developed and implemented	• **ISO/IEC 27001:2013** A.12.6.1, A.18.2.2 • **NIST SP 800-53 Rev. 4** RA-3, RA-5, SI-2
	Maintenance (PR.MA): Maintenance and repairs of industrial control and information system components is performed consistent with policies and procedures.	**PR.MA-1:** Maintenance and repair of organizational assets is performed and logged in a timely manner, with approved and controlled tools	• **COBIT 5** BAI09.03 • **ISA 62443-2-1:2009** 4.3.3.3.7 • **ISO/IEC 27001:2013** A.11.1.2, A.11.2.4, A.11.2.5 • **NIST SP 800-53 Rev. 4** MA-2, MA-3, MA-5
		PR.MA-2: Remote maintenance of organizational assets is approved, logged, and performed in a manner that prevents unauthorized access	• **COBIT 5** DSS05.04 • **ISA 62443-2-1:2009** 4.3.3.6.5, 4.3.3.6.6, 4.3.3.6.7, 4.4.4.6.8 • **ISO/IEC 27001:2013** A.11.2.4, A.15.1.1, A.15.2.1

Function	Category	Subcategory	Informative References
	Protective Technology (PR.PT): Technical security solutions are managed to ensure the security and resilience of systems and assets, consistent with related policies, procedures, and agreements.	**PR.PT-1:** Audit/log records are determined, documented, implemented, and reviewed in accordance with policy	• **NIST SP 800-53 Rev. 4** MA-4 • **CCS CSC** 14 • **COBIT 5** APO11.04 • **ISA 62443-2-1:2009** 4.3.3.3.9, 4.3.3.5.8, 4.3.4.4.7, 4.4.2.1, 4.4.2.2, 4.4.2.4 • **ISA 62443-3-3:2013** SR 2.8, SR 2.9, SR 2.10, SR 2.11, SR 2.12 • **ISO/IEC 27001:2013** A.12.4.1, A.12.4.2, A.12.4.3, A.12.4.4, A.12.7.1 • **NIST SP 800-53 Rev. 4** AU Family
		PR.PT-2: Removable media is protected and its use restricted according to policy	• **COBIT 5** DSS05.02, APO13.01 • **ISA 62443-3-3:2013** SR 2.3 • **ISO/IEC 27001:2013** A.8.2.2, A.8.2.3, A.8.3.1, A.8.3.3, A.11.2.9 • **NIST SP 800-53 Rev. 4** MP-2, MP-4, MP-5, MP-7
		PR.PT-3: Access to systems and assets is controlled, incorporating the principle of least functionality	• **COBIT 5** DSS05.02 • **ISA 62443-2-1:2009** 4.3.3.5.1, 4.3.3.5.2, 4.3.3.5.3, 4.3.3.5.4, 4.3.3.5.5, 4.3.3.5.6, 4.3.3.5.7, 4.3.3.5.8, 4.3.3.6.1, 4.3.3.6.2, 4.3.3.6.3, 4.3.3.6.4, 4.3.3.6.5, 4.3.3.6.6, 4.3.3.6.7, 4.3.3.6.8, 4.3.3.6.9, 4.3.3.7.1, 4.3.3.7.2, 4.3.3.7.3, 4.3.3.7.4 • **ISA 62443-3-3:2013** SR 1.1, SR 1.2, SR 1.3, SR 1.4, SR 1.5, SR 1.6, SR 1.7, SR 1.8, SR 1.9, SR 1.10, SR 1.11, SR 1.12, SR 1.13, SR 2.1, SR 2.2, SR 2.3, SR 2.4, SR 2.5, SR 2.6, SR 2.7 • **ISO/IEC 27001:2013** A.9.1.2 • **NIST SP 800-53 Rev. 4** AC-3, CM-7
		PR.PT-4: Communications and control networks are protected	• **CCS CSC** 7 • **COBIT 5** DSS05.02, APO13.01 • **ISA 62443-3-3:2013** SR 3.1, SR 3.5, SR 3.8, SR 4.1, SR 4.3, SR 5.1, SR 5.2, SR 5.3, SR 7.1,

Function	Category	Subcategory	Informative References
DETECT (DE)		DE.AE-1: A baseline of network operations and expected data flows for users and systems is established and managed	• ISO/IEC 27001:2013 A.13.1.1, A.13.2.1 • NIST SP 800-53 Rev. 4 AC-4, AC-17, AC-18, CP-8, SC-7
	Anomalies and Events (DE.AE): Anomalous activity is detected in a timely manner and the potential impact of events is understood.	DE.AE-2: Detected events are analyzed to understand attack targets and methods	• SR 7.6 • COBIT 5 DSS03.01 • ISA 62443-2-1:2009 4.4.3.3 • NIST SP 800-53 Rev. 4 AC-4, CA-3, CM-2, SI-4
		DE.AE-3: Event data are aggregated and correlated from multiple sources and sensors	• ISA 62443-2-1:2009 4.3.4.5.6, 4.3.4.5.7, 4.3.4.5.8 • ISA 62443-3-3:2013 SR 2.8, SR 2.9, SR 2.10, SR 2.11, SR 2.12, SR 3.9, SR 6.1, SR 6.2 • ISO/IEC 27001:2013 A.16.1.1, A.16.1.4 • NIST SP 800-53 Rev. 4 AU-6, CA-7, IR-4, SI-4
		DE.AE-4: Impact of events is determined	• ISA 62443-3-3:2013 SR 6.1 • NIST SP 800-53 Rev. 4 AU-6, CA-7, IR-4, IR-5, IR-8, SI-4
		DE.AE-5: Incident alert thresholds are established	• COBIT 5 APO12.06 • NIST SP 800-53 Rev. 4 CP-2, IR-4, RA-3, SI-4
	Security Continuous Monitoring (DE.CM): The information system and assets are monitored at discrete intervals to identify cybersecurity events and verify the effectiveness of protective measures.	DE.CM-1: The network is monitored to detect potential cybersecurity events	• COBIT 5 APO12.06 • ISA 62443-2-1:2009 4.2.3.10 • NIST SP 800-53 Rev. 4 IR-4, IR-5, IR-8
		DE.CM-2: The physical environment is	• CCS CSC 14, 16 • COBIT 5 DSS05.07 • ISA 62443-3-3:2013 SR 6.2 • NIST SP 800-53 Rev. 4 AC-2, AU-12, CA-7, CM-3, SC-5, SC-7, SI-4 • ISA 62443-2-1:2009 4.3.3.3.8

Function	Category	Subcategory	Informative References
		monitored to detect potential cybersecurity events	• **NIST SP 800-53 Rev. 4** CA-7, PE-3, PE-6, PE-20
		DE.CM-3: Personnel activity is monitored to detect potential cybersecurity events	• **ISA 62443-3-3:2013** SR 6.2 • **ISO/IEC 27001:2013** A.12.4.1 • **NIST SP 800-53 Rev. 4** AC-2, AU-12, AU-13, CA-7, CM-10, CM-11
		DE.CM-4: Malicious code is detected	• **CCS CSC** 5 • **COBIT 5** DSS05.01 • **ISA 62443-2-1:2009** 4.3.4.3.8 • **ISA 62443-3-3:2013** SR 3.2 • **ISO/IEC 27001:2013** A.12.2.1 • **NIST SP 800-53 Rev. 4** SI-3
		DE.CM-5: Unauthorized mobile code is detected	• **ISA 62443-3-3:2013** SR 2.4 • **ISO/IEC 27001:2013** A.12.5.1 • **NIST SP 800-53 Rev. 4** SC-18, SI-4. SC-44
		DE.CM-6: External service provider activity is monitored to detect potential cybersecurity events	• **COBIT 5** APO07.06 • **ISO/IEC 27001:2013** A.14.2.7, A.15.2.1 • **NIST SP 800-53 Rev. 4** CA-7, PS-7, SA-4, SA-9, SI-4
		DE.CM-7: Monitoring for unauthorized personnel, connections, devices, and software is performed	• **NIST SP 800-53 Rev. 4** AU-12, CA-7, CM-3, CM-8, PE-3, PE-6, PE-20, SI4
		DE.CM-8: Vulnerability scans are performed	• **COBIT 5** BAI03.10 • **ISA 62443-2-1:2009** 4.2.3.1, 4.2.3.7 • **ISO/IEC 27001:2013** A.12.6.1 • **NIST SP 800-53 Rev. 4** RA-5
	Detection Processes (DE.DP): Detection processes and procedures are maintained and tested to ensure timely and	**DE.DP-1:** Roles and responsibilities for detection are well defined to ensure accountability	• **CCS CSC** 5 • **COBIT 5** DSS05.01 • **ISA 62443-2-1:2009** 4.4.3.1 • **ISO/IEC 27001:2013** A.6.1.1

Function	Category	Subcategory	Informative References
	adequate awareness of anomalous events.	**DE.DP-2:** Detection activities comply with all applicable requirements	• **NIST SP 800-53 Rev. 4** CA-2, CA-7, PM-14 • **ISA 62443-2-1:2009** 4.4.3.2 • **ISO/IEC 27001:2013** A.18.1.4 • **NIST SP 800-53 Rev. 4** CA-2, CA-7, PM-14, SI-4
		DE.DP-3: Detection processes are tested	• **COBIT 5** APO13.02 • **ISA 62443-2-1:2009** 4.4.3.2 • **ISA 62443-3-3:2013** SR 3.3 • **ISO/IEC 27001:2013** A.14.2.8 • **NIST SP 800-53 Rev. 4** CA-2, CA-7, PE-3, PM-14, SI-3, SI-4
		DE.DP-4: Event detection information is communicated to appropriate parties	• **COBIT 5** APO12.06 • **ISA 62443-2-1:2009** 4.3.4.5.9 • **ISA 62443-3-3:2013** SR 6.1 • **ISO/IEC 27001:2013** A.16.1.2 • **NIST SP 800-53 Rev. 4** AU-6, CA-2, CA-7, RA-5, SI-4
		DE.DP-5: Detection processes are continuously improved	• **COBIT 5** APO11.06, DSS04.05 • **ISA 62443-2-1:2009** 4.4.3.4 • **ISO/IEC 27001:2013** A.16.1.6 • **NIST SP 800-53 Rev. 4**, CA-2, CA-7, PL-2, RA-5, SI-4, PM-14

Function	Category	Subcategory	Informative References
RESPOND (RS)	**Response Planning (RS.RP):** Response processes and procedures are executed and maintained, to ensure timely response to detected cybersecurity events.	**RS.RP-1:** Response plan is executed during or after an event	• **COBIT 5** BAI01.10 • CCS CSC 18 • **ISA 62443-2-1:2009** 4.3.4.5.1 • **ISO/IEC 27001:2013** A.16.1.5 • **NIST SP 800-53 Rev. 4** CP-2, CP-10, IR-4, IR-8
	Communications (RS.CO): Response activities are coordinated with internal and external stakeholders, as appropriate, to include external support from law enforcement agencies.	**RS.CO-1:** Personnel know their roles and order of operations when a response is needed	• **ISA 62443-2-1:2009** 4.3.4.5.2, 4.3.4.5.3, 4.3.4.5.4 • **ISO/IEC 27001:2013** A.6.1.1, A.16.1.1 • **NIST SP 800-53 Rev. 4** CP-2, CP-3, IR-3, IR-8
		RS.CO-2: Events are reported consistent with established criteria	• **ISA 62443-2-1:2009** 4.3.4.5.5 • **ISO/IEC 27001:2013** A.6.1.3, A.16.1.2 • **NIST SP 800-53 Rev. 4** AU-6, IR-6, IR-8
		RS.CO-3: Information is shared consistent with response plans	• **ISA 62443-2-1:2009** 4.3.4.5.2 • **ISO/IEC 27001:2013** A.16.1.2 • **NIST SP 800-53 Rev. 4** CA-2, CA-7, CP-2, IR-4, IR-8, PE-6, RA-5, SI-4
		RS.CO-4: Coordination with stakeholders occurs consistent with response plans	• **ISA 62443-2-1:2009** 4.3.4.5.5 • **NIST SP 800-53 Rev. 4** CP-2, IR-4, IR-8
		RS.CO-5: Voluntary information sharing occurs with external stakeholders to achieve broader cybersecurity situational awareness	• **NIST SP 800-53 Rev. 4** PM-15, SI-5
	Analysis (RS.AN): Analysis is conducted to ensure adequate response and support recovery activities.	**RS.AN-1:** Notifications from detection systems are investigated	• **COBIT 5** DSS02.07 • **ISA 62443-2-1:2009** 4.3.4.5.6, 4.3.4.5.7, 4.3.4.5.8 • **ISA 62443-3-3:2013** SR 6.1 • **ISO/IEC 27001:2013** A.12.4.1, A.12.4.3, A.16.1.5 • **NIST SP 800-53 Rev. 4** AU-6, CA-7, IR-4, IR-

Function	Category	Subcategory	Informative References
		RS.AN-2: The impact of the incident is understood	• 5, PE-6, SI-4 • **ISA 62443-2-1:2009** 4.3.4.5.6, 4.3.4.5.7, 4.3.4.5.8 • **ISO/IEC 27001:2013** A.16.1.6 • **NIST SP 800-53 Rev. 4** CP-2, IR-4
		RS.AN-3: Forensics are performed	• **ISA 62443-3-3:2013** SR 2.8, SR 2.9, SR 2.10, SR 2.11, SR 2.12, SR 3.9, SR 6.1 • **ISO/IEC 27001:2013** A.16.1.7 • **NIST SP 800-53 Rev. 4** AU-7, IR-4
		RS.AN-4: Incidents are categorized consistent with response plans	• **ISA 62443-2-1:2009** 4.3.4.5.6 • **ISO/IEC 27001:2013** A.16.1.4 • **NIST SP 800-53 Rev. 4** CP-2, IR-4, IR-5, IR-8
	Mitigation (RS.MI): Activities are performed to prevent expansion of an event, mitigate its effects, and eradicate the incident.	**RS.MI-1:** Incidents are contained	• **ISA 62443-2-1:2009** 4.3.4.5.6 • **ISA 62443-3-3:2013** SR 5.1, SR 5.2, SR 5.4 • **ISO/IEC 27001:2013** A.16.1.5 • **NIST SP 800-53 Rev. 4** IR-4
		RS.MI-2: Incidents are mitigated	• **ISA 62443-2-1:2009** 4.3.4.5.6, 4.3.4.5.10 • **ISO/IEC 27001:2013** A.12.2.1, A.16.1.5 • **NIST SP 800-53 Rev. 4** IR-4
		RS.MI-3: Newly identified vulnerabilities are mitigated or documented as accepted risks	• **ISO/IEC 27001:2013** A.12.6.1 • **NIST SP 800-53 Rev. 4** CA-7, RA-3, RA-5
	Improvements (RS.IM): Organizational response activities are improved by incorporating lessons learned from current and previous detection/response activities.	**RS.IM-1:** Response plans incorporate lessons learned	• **COBIT 5** BAI01.13 • **ISA 62443-2-1:2009** 4.3.4.5.10, 4.4.3.4 • **ISO/IEC 27001:2013** A.16.1.6 • **NIST SP 800-53 Rev. 4** CP-2, IR-4, IR-8
		RS.IM-2: Response strategies are updated	• **NIST SP 800-53 Rev. 4** CP-2, IR-4, IR-8
RECOVER (RC)	**Recovery Planning (RC.RP):** Recovery processes and procedures are executed and maintained to ensure timely	**RC.RP-1:** Recovery plan is executed during or after an event	• **CCS CSC** 8 • **COBIT 5** DSS02.05, DSS03.04 • **ISO/IEC 27001:2013** A.16.1.5

Function	Category	Subcategory	Informative References
	restoration of systems or assets affected by cybersecurity events.		• **NIST SP 800-53 Rev. 4** CP-10, IR-4, IR-8
	Improvements (RC.IM): Recovery planning and processes are improved by incorporating lessons learned into future activities.	**RC.IM-1:** Recovery plans incorporate lessons learned	• **COBIT 5** BAI05.07 • **ISA 62443-2-1:2009** 4.4.3.4 • **NIST SP 800-53 Rev. 4** CP-2, IR-4, IR-8
		RC.IM-2: Recovery strategies are updated	• **COBIT 5** BAI07.08 • **NIST SP 800-53 Rev. 4** CP-2, IR-4, IR-8
	Communications (RC.CO): Restoration activities are coordinated with internal and external parties, such as coordinating centers, Internet Service Providers, owners of attacking systems, victims, other CSIRTs, and vendors.	**RC.CO-1:** Public relations are managed	• **COBIT 5** EDM03.02
		RC.CO-2: Reputation after an event is repaired	• **COBIT 5** MEA03.02
		RC.CO-3: Recovery activities are communicated to internal stakeholders and executive and management teams	• **NIST SP 800-53 Rev. 4** CP-2, IR-4

Information regarding Informative References described in Appendix A may be found at the following locations:

- Control Objectives for Information and Related Technology (COBIT): http://www.isaca.org/COBIT/Pages/default.aspx
- Council on CyberSecurity (CCS) Top 20 Critical Security Controls (CSC): http://www.counciloncybersecurity.org
- ANSI/ISA-62443-2-1 (99.02.01)-2009, *Security for Industrial Automation and Control Systems: Establishing an Industrial Automation and Control Systems Security Program:* http://www.isa.org/Template.cfm?Section=Standards8&Template=/Ecommerce/ProductDisplay.cfm&ProductID=10243
  ANSI/ISA-62443-3-3 (99.03.03)-2013, *Security for Industrial Automation and Control Systems: System Security Requirements and Security Levels:* http://www.isa.org/Template.cfm?Section=Standards2&template=/Ecommerce/ProductDisplay.cfm&ProductID=13420
- ISO/IEC 27001, *Information technology -- Security techniques -- Information security management systems -- Requirements:* http://www.iso.org/iso/home/store/catalogue_ics/catalogue_detail_ics.htm?csnumber=54534
- NIST SP 800-53 Rev. 4: NIST Special Publication 800-53 Revision 4, *Security and Privacy Controls for Federal Information Systems and Organizations*, April 2013 (including updates as of January 15, 2014). http://dx.doi.org/10.6028/NIST.SP.800-53r4.

Mappings between the Framework Core Subcategories and the specified sections in the Informative References represent a general correspondence and are not intended to definitively determine whether the specified sections in the Informative References provide the desired Subcategory outcome.

Appendix B: Glossary

This appendix defines selected terms used in the publication.

Category	The subdivision of a Function into groups of cybersecurity outcomes, closely tied to programmatic needs and particular activities. Examples of Categories include "Asset Management," "Access Control," and "Detection Processes."
Critical Infrastructure	Systems and assets, whether physical or virtual, so vital to the United States that the incapacity or destruction of such systems and assets would have a debilitating impact on cybersecurity, national economic security, national public health or safety, or any combination of those matters.
Cybersecurity	The process of protecting information by preventing, detecting, and responding to attacks.
Cybersecurity Event	A cybersecurity change that may have an impact on organizational operations (including mission, capabilities, or reputation).
Detect (function)	Develop and implement the appropriate activities to identify the occurrence of a cybersecurity event.
Framework	A risk-based approach to reducing cybersecurity risk composed of three parts: the Framework Core, the Framework Profile, and the Framework Implementation Tiers. Also known as the "Cybersecurity Framework."
Framework Core	A set of cybersecurity activities and references that are common across critical infrastructure sectors and are organized around particular outcomes. The Framework Core comprises four types of elements: Functions, Categories, Subcategories, and Informative References.
Framework Implementation Tier	A lens through which to view the characteristics of an organization's approach to risk—how an organization views cybersecurity risk and the processes in place to manage that risk.
Framework Profile	A representation of the outcomes that a particular system or organization has selected from the Framework Categories and Subcategories.
Function	One of the main components of the Framework. Functions provide the highest level of structure for organizing basic cybersecurity activities into Categories and Subcategories. The five functions are Identify,

Protect, Detect, Respond, and Recover.

Identify (function)	Develop the organizational understanding to manage cybersecurity risk to systems, assets, data, and capabilities.
Informative Reference	A specific section of standards, guidelines, and practices common among critical infrastructure sectors that illustrates a method to achieve the outcomes associated with each Subcategory.
Mobile Code	A program (e.g., script, macro, or other portable instruction) that can be shipped unchanged to a heterogeneous collection of platforms and executed with identical semantics.
Protect (function)	Develop and implement the appropriate safeguards to ensure delivery of critical infrastructure services.
Privileged User	A user that is authorized (and, therefore, trusted) to perform security-relevant functions that ordinary users are not authorized to perform.
Recover (function)	Develop and implement the appropriate activities to maintain plans for resilience and to restore any capabilities or services that were impaired due to a cybersecurity event.
Respond (function)	Develop and implement the appropriate activities to take action regarding a detected cybersecurity event.
Risk	A measure of the extent to which an entity is threatened by a potential circumstance or event, and typically a function of: (i) the adverse impacts that would arise if the circumstance or event occurs; and (ii) the likelihood of occurrence.
Risk Management	The process of identifying, assessing, and responding to risk.
Subcategory	The subdivision of a Category into specific outcomes of technical and/or management activities. Examples of Subcategories include "External information systems are catalogued," "Data-at-rest is protected," and "Notifications from detection systems are investigated."

Appendix C: Acronyms

This appendix defines selected acronyms used in the publication.

CCS	Council on CyberSecurity
COBIT	Control Objectives for Information and Related Technology
DCS	Distributed Control System
DHS	Department of Homeland Security
EO	Executive Order
ICS	Industrial Control Systems
IEC	International Electrotechnical Commission
IR	Interagency Report
ISA	International Society of Automation
ISAC	Information Sharing and Analysis Center
ISO	International Organization for Standardization
IT	Information Technology
NIST	National Institute of Standards and Technology
RFI	Request for Information
RMP	Risk Management Process
SCADA	Supervisory Control and Data Acquisition
SP	Special Publication